# From the Footplate

## J R Carter

ABOVE: The early morning coal traffic is on the move: the first train from Speakmans Sidings Leigh to Patricroft, headed and banked by Stanier class 8F 2-8-0s. As the train passes Jacksons Sidings the banker is really digging in, with obvious clear signals. To the left of shot are three stop blocks, Jacksons Sidings signal box and 9F No. 92019 with steam from her safety valves drifting into the exhaust of the train engine. While the guard was going around our train, there was ample time after putting a good round of coal on the fire, to wander towards Leigh and obtain a good photographic position on the stop block nearest to the main line, with the certain knowledge that the second coal train was only the passage of an eastbound DMU away.

FRONT COVER: Stanier 4-6-2 No. 46254 *City of Stoke-on-Trent,* with steam raiser and shovel prominent, simmers quietly at Crewe North Shed, believed prior to a Royal Train working.

REAR COVER: Class 9F No. 92019, Driver Cliff Davies in the cab, stands by to work a coal train from Jackson's sidings, Tyldesley, while fireman Carter does some camera work! The rest of the story is inside the book.

ISBN 0-906899-44-3. First Published 1990

© J. R. Carter and Atlantic Transport Publishers.

Published by

**Atlantic Transport Publishers**
**Trevithick House . West End**
**Penryn . Cornwall TR10 8HE**

Designed by Barnabus Design & Print . Truro . Cornwall.     Typeset by TypeStyle . Truro . Cornwall
Printed by Century Litho . Penryn . Cornwall.     Bound by Booths Bookbinders . Penryn . Cornwall

# CONTENTS

# DEDICATION

I would like to take this opportunity to thank my long suffering wife Irene for typing the manuscript of this book and coping with my fascination with steam locomotives during thirty one years of marriage. We met at the age of sixteen and during our courting days, as I am sure most of us will admit, we took walks through the fields on long summer evenings; but our romantic strolls were always conveniently close to some sort of railway line! Irene lived in St. Helens, north of the Liverpool Lime St-Manchester main line, I lived roughly equal distance to the south and one engine we used to see regularly was Jubilee No. 45581 *Bihar and Orissa;* Irene still remembers the name and number.

On our wedding day, whilst waiting outside St. Nicholas church, my brother Colin and I heard the unmistakable sound of a Stanier whistle in the distance towards Lea Green and in the rush to get trackside to see the passage of the train, we almost fell into an open grave. Happy omen – the loco was No. 45581!

Throughout our marriage I have pulled all sorts of stunts to get my legs out of the house to photograph steam locomotives. There were times when Irene accompanied me and times when she didn't; there were also times when it was inconvenient. However, throughout the years she has taken it all in her stride, and at times actually enjoyed the sight and sound of big engines in action. I therefore think it is appropriate to dedicate this book to my wife Irene for all the help and encouragement she has given me over the years.

# INTRODUCTION

Some considerable time has passed since the publication of my last book (Footplate Cameraman – Ian Allan) in which my friend David Jenkinson wrote the foreword. He was at that time in a high position at The National Railway Museum at York and active with the operation of Stanier Pacific No. 46229 *Duchess of Hamilton.* We met on several occasions when the 'Duchess' was in action on BR metals and on one occasion he made it right for me to shoot her at nightime outside the annexe at York. He has now left the security of the NRM in favour of the publishing business, and is one of the few people who could have persuaded me to have a go at another book. A few informal conversations over the telephone finally led to a meeting in the British Rail Staff Association club at Manchester Piccadilly on 8th February 1990. After a railway dinner (ie: steak pie and chips and a few pints of ale) and armed with a box of slides and a portable viewer, we examined the contents of around 200 thirty-year old slides in no particular order. The locations ranged from Patricroft, Crewe, Edge Hill, North West coast main line and a few excursions onto GW and SR metals.

The reality which emerged was an incomplete box of odds and sods plus a few footplate tales to tell; and it has proved to be difficult to establish a theme to run through a book when the contents were photographed some thirty years ago purely for my own pleasure. I had no idea how the railway scene would have changed during that period of time but it soon became apparent that David and I were thinking along the same lines: my experiences on and around the lines to Patricroft.

Firing in the freight links at Patricroft on Derby Class 4s, Crewe Super Ds, and Stanier 8Fs was not as satisfying as firing big 'Scots', 'Jubilees', 'Patriots', etc., in the passenger links and the difference as a steam photographer was clear. When working on main line steam jobs, most of the time you had two hands on the shovel, operating injectors, dragging the coal down, reducing the size with a coal pick to fit into the firebox, operating the water scoop, putting the bag in, hooking on and off, looking out for signals, etc.; there was little time to use a camera. At places such as Leeds, turning the loco on the man-powered turn table took most of the time and it was no better at Liverpool Lime St. After hooking off, the pilot engine would drag your train off, but when released your next move would be to work another train of empty stock to Edge Hill carriage sidings and finally, light engine onto the sheds, after emptying the smoke box, cleaning the fire, coaling, watering and turning the engine. Then and only then, there would be some time, light permitting, to take photographs.

After passing out for driving steam locomotives in August 1962, I was promoted from firing main line express passenger trains to firing coal and freight trains in a new grade (passed fireman). In the freight links, 'passed' men had fairly comfortable booking-on times and were rarely far away from the depot; one could book on for firing duties and be promoted to driver for the day, on any job from a 'Jinty' on the up-side shunt, to a big 'Scot' on an express passenger train and to any location according to your route card; but as a young hand passed fireman, these driving turns were few and far between.

The pace in the freight links was much slower, with long periods of time spent standing around in various sidings. It was during the early to mid 1960s, partly to relieve the boredom after working in the top passenger links, that I decided to make the best of a bad job with my camera. There were few opportunities to photograph my beloved Stanier Pacifics, so with time in hand between working various coal trains, I turned the camera onto the locomotives and trains that, until then, had least interested me. The fullness of time has proved this to have been a fruitful exercise, as photographs of steam hauled coal trains in the Leigh/Tyldesley and Patricroft area are now a little thin on the ground. In those days not one would cast a glance at the passage of a coal train, apart from some irate fist-clenching housewives pegging their washing out; with them, footplate crews were not very popular for obvious reasons.

A good starting point for the book would be to go back in time to a cold spring morning at Patricroft depot in 1964 when, as a passed man, I had a booking on time at only 4.30 am, with high hopes of getting a driving turn in; but as fate would have it I was teamed up as a fireman with driver Cliff Davies to work a special coal train. We were given class 9F No. 92019 to prepare and to

quote shed foreman, Billy Graham: "Get off the shed as soon as possible if not sooner". Little time to spare and bad light provided no photographic opportunities before departing, light engine, to Jacksons Sidings Tyldesley.

We arrived in good time but were shunted to one side while the NCB loco from Gin Pit was busy backing up loaded coal wagons on to our brake van. The completion of the operation took some considerable time, quite long enough to have a brew and a bit of breakfast. By the time we backed up on our train, the sun was up and the early morning coal traffic from Speakmans Sidings Leigh was on the move; but the early morning DMUs had also started, so signalmen on the branch gave them top priority. As we were waiting for a clear road, there was ample time to take the first set of slides to appear in the book including those on the title page and rear cover.

I now live virtually on the doorstep of the old track bed and find it hard to believe there was ever a colliery head gear, pit and mill chimneys, smouldering slag heaps, steam locomotives and coal-fired houses, all belching smoke out into the atmosphere. Today all one hears about is lead-free petrol, power stations, acid rain and aerosol sprays, etc., damaging the ozone layer. I think the damage to the environment was done long ago.

The area where we started that spring morning during during 1964 with No. 92019 is now more like a country park; the pits have gone, slag heaps have been flattened and landscaped, while Fred Dibnah (celebrated TV steeplejack and chimney feller) has also made his mark on the skyline by removing some of it! There are still some signs of the old track bed but one has to know where to look for them.

The bulk of coal traffic was moved during mornings and the engines that moved the coal eventually found their way back to Patricroft sheds for servicing, ready for their next turn of duty; some engines would be back in traffic within the hour, others would simmer away until the following morning. Some of the slides in this book show Stanier 8Fs at the depot during servicing, photographed from a well chosen and somewhat dodgy position up the coal shute. Enthusiasts who enjoy technical details of certain locomotives will no doubt be disappointed.

Having worked for almost thirty years in the footplate grade from cleaning, firing and driving a wide variety of steam locomotives, and surviving the transition to diesel traction while driving them on the main line as well as on shunting jobs, one picks up some technical points. But the idea of this book is to divert the mind to the artistic side of working steam locomotives in locations off the beaten track and away from those other lines and depots well known to most enthusiasts.

Working in the footplate grade these days is totally different from when I started work for British Railways in 1952. I was fortunate enough to progress from an engine spotter to engine cleaner as a fifteen year old school leaver at Sutton Oak sheds, and eventually passed the steam engine driving test at Patricroft some ten years later. It was seventeen years before I became a booked driver at Newton Heath – a long apprentice by any standards. Now, young lads drive big diesels without having to even clean them. My oldest son David proves to be a good example of how the passage to the driver's seat has changed. He started work for British Rail as a second man at Manchester Victoria in October 1985; by October 1988 he was a booked driver at Warrington and now drives big diesels over some of the routes on which I fired steam engines over thirty years ago. To David and all young hand drivers I wish the best of luck, (some will need it). AWS, colour light signalling, good vision on modern traction and air-braked trains all make the job somewhat easier. But make no mistake, when seeing young lads at the control of main line diesels, remember they have all gone though a tough period of training and some fell by the wayside. I am sure that those who have made it will become good drivers.

Although retired through ill health, I occasionally turn out to photograph certain preserved steam locomotives and have a good crack with other steam cameramen; but most of all I enjoy the company of my old footplate pals when, over a few pints of ale in the Manchester railway clubs, we can reminisce over the days when we all worked 'From the Footplate'. These men were mostly unsung heroes – and this is my modest little tribute to them.

Jim Carter, Leigh, 1990.

Opposite: This shot taken from the stop block, described on the title page, shows Stanier 8F No. 48491 with a full coal train banked by 8F No. 48636 attacking the gradient to Tyldesley. The distant signal is at caution; that presents a major problem for both drivers, more so for the bank engine driver as his vision is impaired. In this case the distant signal was on while a local passenger train from Manchester to Wigan was cleared from Tyldesley station.

Right, upper: Fortunately by the time No. 48491 passed the camera position, the driver could see home and distant signals showing a clear road through Tyldesley. Drivers needed a good run at the bank with loaded loose coupled coal trains with thirty odd wagons or more; it was hard enough to make it up the incline without a signal check, even more so on wet and greasy rails. When the inevitable happened it was not easy to stop a heavy coal train with a banker to the rear and then hold the train on the gradient preventing the wagons running back. A further problem was to get the train on the move again; more often than not the assistance of another locomotive would be required to restart a train stopped on the bank. After a period of time with engines slipping to a stand, causing delays to local passenger traffic due to signal checks, it soon became common practice for signalmen at Speakmans Sidings signal box to hold heavy coal trains on that section of line until there was a guaranteed clear road through Jacksons and Tyldesley.

Right, lower: The driver of the bank engine on 8F 48636 having seen clear signals gets stuck in with this second in the procession of early morning coal trains from Speakmans up the comparatively short incline to Tyldesley.

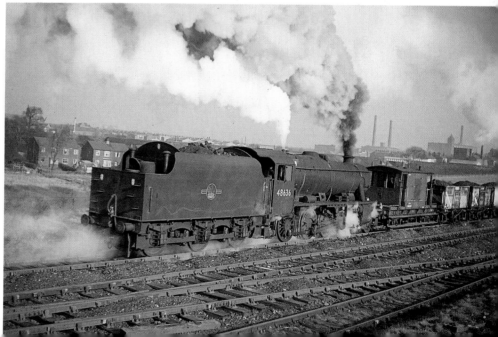

A general view of the area showing exhaust and smoke from bank engine No. 48636, our 9F No. 92019 creeping round Jacksons Sidings signal box and St. Georges colliery to the right background. Some of the NCB trackwork has been lifted, visible to the bottom right of shot.

Double-banking: In this view, taken from just beyond the signal box visible in the previous picture, Class 8F No. 48770 and an unidentified BR Class 5MT 4-6-0 give a double dose of rear-end assistance to yet another heavy coal train as we wait our turn for the road.

After the passage of the second coal train, steam from the safety valves of No. 48636 is still visible in the background as she tops the bank, while our 9F drifts down the incline to join BR from NCB metals heading west from Jacksons Sidings. The bridge that carries the line from Manchester to Wigan is visible in the background to the left of No. 92019.

No. 92019 photographed on the same trip, this time during a signal check at Kenyon Junction to await the passage of a Liverpool-Manchester express. The main line is visible in the foreground and the one time busy but now almost deserted sidings look in need of a visit from the weed killing train.

After 'gassing up' (raising steam pressure for those who want the proper formal term) Stanier 8F No. 48322 waits in Jackson Sidings for a signal to propel our train westwards onto the main line. My driver on this occasion, Tommy Swift is doing a bit of posing out of the cab window on the fireman's side of our engine.

As with several views in this book, I have included this picture not just to show the kind of trains we worked and the general conditions of the time, but also to give some detailed information to modelmakers.

After coming to a stand on the main line (wrong road) No. 48322 is ready to go with bank engine No. 48720 in position to assist us up the incline to Tyldesley, after the passage of a Liverpool Lime St.-Manchester Exchange DMU.

Opposite: On the same trip is a view from the footplate of No. 48322 looking back down the train. Bank engine No. 48720 is digging in, Jacksons Sidings and the signal box are visible to left of shot and the track work in the foreground which disappears under our train is the line to Wigan Atherton Bag Lane and Bolton Great Moor Street.

A shot from the bank engine on the sam
gradient, shifting yet another coal train t
Tyldesley; both footplate shots show th
distant signal for Tyldesley at caution.

tanier 8F No. 48720 propels the heaviest art of her train into the NCB sidings near orsley; in the background is the signal ox. The rest of the train stands with the rake in the guard's van firmly screwed on nd the brakes on the remaining wagons ell pinned down to prevent a runaway on is falling gradient. After completion of this ovement the locomotive would back up nd take the train as far as Patricroft North dings, from where it would then proceed ght engine onto Patricroft sheds for ervicing.

North Staffordshire Railway 0-6-2 side nk No. 2 waits for the coal wagons to be abled in the NCB sidings (see left and ght background of shot). After the depar-re of No. 48720, No. 2, with the assis-nce of an ex-WD 0-6-0 saddle tank will anoeuvre the train into the washing plant Sandholes Pit. This was a rare case of an gine scheduled for preservation being ut to work again by its owners after being painted in its 'museum' livery.

In the Leigh, Tyldesley, Atherton, Astley an Walkden area, the NCB had more track work, mile for mile, than BR. It was possib to get from Astley Moss (off the ma Liverpool-Manchester line) to Ashton field near Bolton entirely on NCB metals. The even had their own workshops at Walkde where they could undertake the complet overhaul of any of their locomotives – a so of equivalent to Crewe, NCB style. Ex LNER Austerity 0-6-0ST *Harry* is seen this shot over the bridge on the A580 Ea Lancashire road near Mossley Commo colliery, heading towards Walkden with train from Boothstown. The cutting and sid ings have now been filled in and a larg housing estate has been built on the site The only sign that there was ever a moder colliery or a busy NCB line are the walls the bridge on the A580 that *Harry* wa about to pass under, one spring afternoo during the early 1960s.

NCB 0-6-0ST *James* propels a train of inte nal wagons over the Bridgewater can towards the BR main line at Astley Mos after being assisted part of the way up th bank by 0-6-0T *Bridgewater,* named afte Lord Bridgewater who was responsible fo the construction of the canal to provide th conveyance of coal and cotton from th various pits and mills in the area, we before any railways were even thought of.

Opposite: Stanier 8F No. 48375 is about rejoin BR metals at Astley Moss with a spe cial coal train from Astley Green colliery Margam in South Wales, with Patricro driver Joe Edwards at the controls.

A clean ex-shops engine was somethin of a rarity on these workings and No. 4837 makes a nice picture with the sunlight glin ing off her fresh paintwork.

# PATRICROFT SHED

Patricroft was my home shed at this time and as I explained in the introduction, I took many views from the top of the coal shute of our engines coming and going. Here are just three of them.

In this first picture, two Stanier 8Fs are back on Patricroft Depot after working early morning coal trains as shed pilot BR Standard Class 3 2-6-2T No. stands by the side of the disposing cabin. While No 48720 makes use of the turntable, an unidentified 8F makes her way towards the new shed (Manchester end) ready for the next turn of duty, possibly a job over the Pennines as the smoke box is facing east.

A view from the top of the coal shute at Patricroft sheds looking East towards Eccles and Manchester showing the top of the roof of the new shed and a BR Class 9F on the ash pit, from whose ash plant I have taken many elevated shots of locomotives on the turntable. Here can be seen BR Class 3 side tank and two 8Fs as a 'Britannia' Pacific departs with a freight from the north sidings and a 350hp Diesel Electric shunter is stabled outside the shunters' cabin in the up sidings.

An unusual view of one of the best Patricroft 8Fs, No. 48720, again shot from the top of the coal shute, smoke box facing West.

I have always liked the challenge of taking locomotive pictures by night and people have often asked me how I do it. Well, in the days when these views were taken there were no such things as electronic flash for the likes of me, so I used to need many a dozen flash bulbs. I would 'set' the view I wanted (and the camera on its tripod) and open the shutter. I then 'painted' the engine with light by letting off a series of flash bulbs in different places to suit my purpose.

I had to walk quickly and soon developed 'asbestos fingers' as a result of removing hot flash bulbs to make way for the next – and since I occasionally set off a few at the rear of the engine to give a bit of back light, I sometimes had to be very careful not to be visible myself.

Of course, I never knew what the results would be like until I got the slides back – and there were many failures – but the good ones were worth the effort and on this page I have included three that I particularly like, taken on my rare visits away from the Manchester area.

Left, above: Peppercorn A2 Pacific No. 60532 *Blue Peter* takes on water at St Rollox shed Glasgow on the Friday night of the 2nd of September 1966 prior to working the last night steam working between Glasgow and Aberdeen.

Left, below: Gresley A4 Pacific No. 60019 *Bittern* also on St. Rollox depot and photographed in the early hours of 3rd September 1966 during an all night cleaning session, so she could look her best when working the last steam hauled passenger train between Glasgow and Aberdeen.

Bulleid Pacifics Nos. 34013 *Okehampton* and 34087 *145 Squadron* again photographed during the early hours while waiting their next turn of duty outside Eastleigh sheds 12th July 1966.

# EDGE HILL

In my opinion Edge Hill shed was second only to Crewe North for photographing big steam locomotives during my steam days, though it wasn't the tidiest depot I have known. At times one could get off an engine around the ash pit and step onto a pile of smouldering ash and clinker in the area of the coal shute and ash pits. Fire irons, cobs of coal and smokebox ash were scattered all over the place but somehow photographically it all added to the atmosphere of the depot.

The reason for my presence at Edge Hill on a Sunday afternoon during 1961 was that driver Tom Jones and myself had brought a Black Five light engine from Patricroft. After disposing of our loco and with no return working, we had more than two hours to kill before the first engine to Lime Street Station was due off the shed – the 4.10 pm London engine. My mate Tom went into the canteen for a brew and to review the Sunday papers but I carefully weighed up the photographic possibilities of the formation of engines at the west end of the shed. One thing was clear, to get any sort of decent photography, No. 46245 *City of London,* had to be moved; as it happened No. 46245 was also the 4.10 pm London engine.

Being early Sunday afternoon there was hardly anybody about apart from a couple of fitters and the steam raiser, who had no objections to me 'gassing up' No. 46245 and also turned a blind eye when the movement took place – he had more than enough to do looking after engines in light steam and lighting up dead engines ready for Monday morning. After spreading the fire and putting a good round of coal on, I did a bit of a tidying-up job in the immediate area, moving fire irons, buffer lamps, tool buckets, etc. Eventually No. 46245 was moved just far enough to reveal another Stanier Pacific No. 46233 *Duchess of Sutherland* and the front end of No. 45552 *Silver Jubilee.* The first view shows the result, with part of 'Jubilee' No. 45583 *Assam* also visible to the right of shot; a wide angle lens would certainly have been useful on this occasion.

The second, nicely lit rear three-quarter
shot shows plenty of detail in the wheels
and valve gear of No. 46233, though even
after my clean-up there is still evidence of
what an untidy depot Edge Hill was. On the
used yard broken pieces from brick arch,
ash and clinker are visible in the foreground, also a steam raiser's shovel; part
of the red tender of another Stanier Pacific

can be seen to the right of shot. Note: It
was common practice to use pieces of
brick arch/fire brick to cover the firebars,
particularly in the back corners of the firebox of Stanier Pacifics, to prevent the early
formation of clinker which would restrict
the air flow.

Finally, in the last view, *City of London*
will soon be on her way to London with the

4.10 pm train from Liverpool Lime Street
station. In this shot she is still 'gassing up'
with tender well cobbed up. To the right,
the tender of No. 45552 is also well coaled;
she had a reputation for bad steaming but I
worked on her regularly in the top passenger links at Patricroft depot (as a fireman)
without any trouble and never had a rough
trip.

We now take a brief look at other parts of Manchester and start with a Stanier Class 4P 2-6-4T No. 42456 as it catches the mid morning sunlight on Platform 14 of Manchester Victoria station, ready to work a local passenger train to Wigan Wallgate.

There is a wealth of what I call 'real' railway detail to be seen in this view. Note, for instance, the tidy stack of destination boards on the platform and the clock faces which were set to indicate departure times. Note too the changed position of the top

lamp iron because of the danger to the crew from the newly introduced overhead electric wires if it had remained in its former position at the top of the door. It also make it easier to reach! This is another of my pictures which I hope will help modelmakers.

Stanier Black Five No. 44756 fitted with Caprotti valve gear and double chimney in rather grubby condition waits to depart from Platform 12 of Manchester Victoria with the 12.45 pm express to Southport; the shape of things to come is visible in the background in the shape of a green-painted Metro-Cammell Diesel Multiple Unit.

Although the steam train carries 'express' headlamps, the coaches were all non-corridors – a bit unusual at this time. The first carriage is to BR design but the second one is of GWR origin.

Stanier 'Jubilee' Class 4-6-0, No. 45647 *Sturdee,* takes the through road at Manchester Exchange with a train of empty stock bound for Ordsall Lane carriage sidings. After arriving on Platform 11 middle, with an express from Leeds, she has been turned onto the through road to by-pass a local passenger train standing at Platform 3 of Exchange station. The connecting platform from the east end of Victoria to the west end of Exchange was the longest platform on BR at the time.

Today, of course, Manchester Exchange is no more and even Manchester Victoria (with which it was linked) has lost some of its services to Manchester Picadilly (formerly London Road).

Gresley LNER Class A4 Pacific No. 60019 *Bittern* was a rare visitor to a Manchester area depot. Here at Stockport Edgeley she receives attention from the Edgeley engine cleaners assisted by some members of the Dinting Railway Society after running light engine from the Scottish Region to work an enthusiasts special the following day. Ladders were much in evidence and as can be seen by comparing the first and second views, the dedicated team finally got the top of the casing clean!

The final picture shows a front end view of No. 60019 *Bittern* soon after arrival at Stockport Edgeley sheds. The support crew worked through the night and I took the opportunity to take another of my 'multiple flash' shots while the work progressed.

We take leave of Manchester for the moment with the sight of an ex-LNWR 'Super D' 0-8-0 No. 49233 wheezing her way on the through road at Manchester Exchange with a freight train from Huddersfield to Ordsall Lane (Salford), with Patricroft driver Peter Lomas visible on the footplate.

This view gives a very good impression of the complexity which was once to be seen in this part of Manchester, with carriage sidings in the background and many freight vehicles even in the station itself. Rumour has it that amongst the many times when goods trains used to traverse the lines between Manchester Victoria and

Exchange, there were occasions when the 'Super D's' got slightly out of control on Miles Platting bank and came through with indecent haste! And this seems a very good way of changing the scene – to Crewe itself where the 'Super Ds' were built.

# CREWE: ITS WORKS AND SHEDS

Crewe Works was probably the most important locomotive repair depot in the whole of Britain and in my time, almost all of the engines on which I worked would be sent there for major repairs. These included examples of one of Crewe's most typical products, the ex-LNWR 0-8-0s.

In this first view, tenderless 'Super D' No. 48895 was photographed outside the erecting shops at Crewe works; beyond the traverser, fitters are hard at work on top of the firebox of a Stanier class 8F.

In the second picture, another ex-LNWR 0-8-0 No. 49335 (official classification G2A), fresh out of the paint shops at Crewe works, was one of the few fitted with a cab on the tender. I did a lot of work on this class cleaning, firing and driving; they were known as 'Super Ds' because they were fitted with superheated boilers, but believe me, they were anything but 'super' and were the most awkward engines I have ever worked on. During an average eight hour shift on the sort of jobs these engines were rostered to work, half would be tender first and in winter, footplatemen would get half frozen, pelted with hail, rain and snow – there were tarpaulin weather sheets provided but they were a waste of time.

The 'Ds' with cabs on the tender seemed to disappear when the weather was bad only to appear again on red hot summer days; then it was the other extreme. The front of the belpaire firebox had no lagging either, which made conditions on the footplate even more uncomfortable. It was hot enough when running but when standing at signals or in the sidings, the heat was unbearable with a cab fitted to the tender and one would get off the footplate as soon as possible. I could go on and on about the shortcomings of this class; in fact I cannot think of one redeeming factor in their favour. To the right of shot is a Stanier 'Pink Five' – the boiler already in primer – waiting her turn to visit the paint shops.

Left, above: Crewe North was always one of my happiest hunting grounds with a camera and in this shot, Stanier Black Five 4-6-0 No. 45338 and Coronation class 4-6-2 No. 46239 *City of Chester*, with part of another Stanier Pacific to the extreme right of shot, all stand in the afternoon sunlight at Crewe North depot. By now, the 'Big Lizzie', as the Coronations were sometimes called has received a diagonal yellow stripe on the cabs – a visible reminder that it could no longer work 'under the wire' south of Crewe.

Left, below: Ex-works 'Britannia' 4-6-2 No. 70047 (the only one of the class never to receive a name) photographed at Crewe North waiting her turn to use the coal shute after working a running-in turn from Shrewsbury. Although ex-shops, it will be noted that No. 700A has been newly repainted without lining – a sign of the changing times.

Opposite: Stanier Pacific No. 46238 *City of Carlisle* is ready to draw up and have her tender topped up with coal. While I was climbing up to my chosen position on the coal shute to take this shot, an unidentified WR 4-6-0 had drifted on to Crewe North sheds behind No. 46238. The smokebox shedplate reveals that No. 46238 was based at her namesake city and she would soon be on her way 'home'.

Opposite: BR three-cylinder Caprotti 4-6-2, No. 71000 *Duke of Gloucester,* takes on water at Crewe North after another miserable trip from the north. The fireman who had worked No. 71000 from Carlisle said to me as he climbed off the footplate: "That's the only time the B------s blown off all day!" Since then, I believe that those dedicated folk who have restored this engine to working order have managed to cure some of its former problems.

A grimy 'Britannia' Pacific, No. 70034 *Thomas Hardy,* simmers away on Crewe South sheds; the steam raiser is having a minute to roll his 'bacca' and can be seen to the left of the tender. For the benefit of those who don't know what a steam raiser's job was, they were firemen who never went off the shed. Their duties were to look after engines in light steam and fire up dead engines after boiler wash-outs and general repairs were completed; passed cleaners

were utilised to do this job when necessary. Some large depots needed more than one steam raiser on each shift to cope with the allocation of locomotives, which varied according to the size of the depot.

In my steam photographing days it was an accepted fact that good railway interest was an excuse for bad camera work and the slides on these two pages prove just that, with the tops of engines cluttered up with electric gantries and a couple of crane jibs in Crewe works. When main line locomotives were out-shopped from Crewe works, it was common practice to drag two or three dead engines onto the South sheds during the afternoon to be fired up for the following day when they travelled light engines (coupled) to Shrewsbury and round the triangle. They would then stand to one side for the examination of axle boxes, valve gear, etc. to check that they were not getting hot, and then go back to Crewe North for further examination before returning into traffic on various local passenger running-in turns.

The slides in this sequence were taken soon after arrival at Crewe North of two 'Scots' and a 'Jubilee'. Unfortunately I was unable to shoot the first 'Scot', but managed to photograph No. 46140 *The Kings Royal Rifle Corps* with the driver still feeling around for hot axle boxes. 'Jubilee' No. 45669 *Fisher* and No. 46140 are seen just prior to being uncoupled with some human activity visible in the shed yard. After being upcoupled, No. 45669 drops down towards the Holyhead end of the shed yard to gain access to the coal shute, ash pit, etc.

'Britannia' pacific No. 70050 *Firth of Clyde* was photographed outside the paint shops at Crewe works but has only received a patched up paint job. The locomotive is fitted with a BR Mk I (D) high sided nine-ton coal capacity tender, complete with coal pusher.

Opposite: Stanier Pacific 46238 *City of Carlisle* has just arrived on Crewe North sheds after working a parcels train in from Carlisle during the summer of 1964. This view was taken on the same occasion as that on page 27.

BR Class 9F No. 92124 and a Stanier class 8F wait to be reunited with their tenders outside the erecting shops at Crewe works.

# LOCOMOTIVE DETAIL

In earlier pages, I have included a few pictures to help modelmakers. Here are a few more, along with some of my own observations about the engines in question.

Right: Some good low lighting shows the Stephenson's link valve gear on Black Five No. 44767 at Patricroft. I fired and drove this engine on several occasions and found her to be stronger and a freer running engine than the rest of a great class of locomotives.

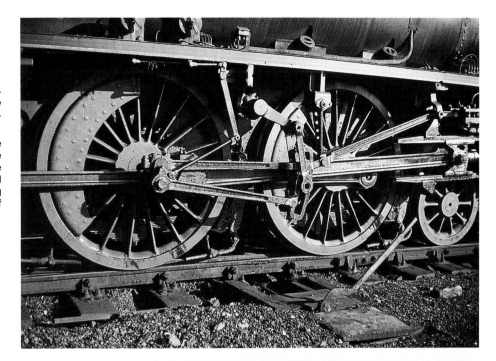

Right: A close up view of a well oiled Caprotti valve gear fitted to BR Class 5MT 4-6-0 No. 73125, shot in the NCB sidings at Astley Green. Patricroft depot inherited more than enough of the Caprotti's from the Western Region, in exchange for our BR Class Fives with Walschaerts valve gear during 1959. The WR locomen didn't like them and Patricroft men liked them even less; they made a lot of noise at the front end but didn't have the equivalent power of Walschaert engines. They were fine when working six coach trains on level roads but give them any hard work to do, although they sounded good, their performance was poor.

Opposite: A view of the chime whistle on a 'Britannia' Pacific cleaned up by J.R.C. 'Britannias' were alright fresh off the works, but after they had done a bit of hard work they became dead rough; the only thing I liked about them was the whistle! In my opinion and experience, the Big Scots were much better locomotives, but I guess I am biassed.

Stanier Black Five No. 45289 is well in her stride as she approaches Warrington Bank Quay station ready to tackle the incline up to the Manchester Ship Canal bridge at Acton Grange with a heavy steel train bound for Crewe. The front end of the 'Super D' that I was firing from Crewe (and the parachute water tank in Frog Hall sidings) can be seen to the left of shot. The second bridge in the background carries the line from Liverpool to Manchester via Widnes and Warrington Central.

'Panned' shots have always been a challenge to me. Most of those which have been published have been in black and white because of the higher film speed, but I did manage the odd one in colour. Here, rebuilt Patriot No. 45526 *Morecambe and Heysham* is running well as she passes through Winwick with a Crewe-Carlisle fast freight train.

Stanier Pacific No. 46225 *Duchess of Gloucester* restarts the 1.30 pm Crewe-Carlisle parcels train from the down slow line to the down fast at Winwick Junction after the clearance of a north bound diesel-hauled express. I had already photographed No. 46225 from the bridge visible in the background and had just enough time to get from bridge to bridge on my motor bike. There was a young engine spotter sitting on a fence with his ABC, so I gave him a 35mm camera and he took this shot. I can be seen at the foot of the signals still with crash helmet on, but I wonder what became of the 'photographer'!

Left: BR Standard ex-Crosti Class No. 92026 in company with another 9F is 'gassing up' on Birkenhead shed, which depot had more than its fair share of 9Fs at that time during the early to mid sixties. They were known to locomen as "Birkenhead Sulzers"! The curious shape of the ex-Crosti engines arose from the removal of their original pre-heat boilers (set below the main boiler) but without much additional modification to the original (upper) unit.

Opposite: In this night shot, Ex works Stanier Class 8F No. 48773 stands outside the east end of Patricroft sheds awaiting her next turn of duty.

Below: By complete contrast with the upper view on this page, a clean 9F No. 92085 with cylinder taps opened, makes her way off the shed light engine to Stanlow to work an oil tank train.

'Battle of Britain' Class Pacific No. 34086, *219 Squadron* blows off and is ready for departure from Waterloo station on 25th May 1965.

Opposite: Another Bullied light Pacific, this time 'West Country' Class No. 34038 *Lynton,* takes on water at Southampton Central station before continuing her jour-

ney to Waterloo. To the left of shot is a B Standard Class 4 which will follow after th departure of the London-bound train whic unusually for this time, was formed fron red not green-painted carriages.

We finish our brief look at the Southern
Region with a suitable link back to the LMR
in the shape of ex-works Stanier Class 8F
2-8-0 No. 48408 in the unusual company of
two Bullied pacifics outside the west end of
Eastleigh sheds soon after being out-
shopped from Eastleigh works on 25th of
May 1965. This particular engine had actually been built by the GWR at Swindon during the war but many other 8Fs were also
built by the SR at the same time.

We end where we began, at Patricroft and another ex-works Stanier 8F; this one had received the full treatment at Crewe works. No. 48158 was photographed from the ash plant at Patricroft sheds, driver Joe Edwards has coupled the locomotive vacuum pipe to the pipe of the vacuum operated motor on the turntable and can be seen to the right of the engine, just about to start the operation; the turntable motor is clearly visible to the right of shot. To work this type of motor you needed enough steam to create 21ins of vacuum – the alternative was to use the old fashioned mangle handle!

Left, upper: 'Unrebuilt 'Patriot' Class 4-6-0 No. 45543 *Home Guard,* allocated to Carnforth, photographed on the turntable at Patricroft shed. There is a fitter to the right of shot waiting for her to be turned and shedded prior to giving her the once-over before going light engine to Manchester Exchange to work the 5.10 pm express to Windermere. No. 45543 was one of the last of the unrebuilt members of the class to work main line trains.

Left, lower: Another shot from the top of the ash plant at Patricroft, the best position to photograph locomotives on the turntable (the only shot of the plant I have appears on page 14). Rebuilt Royal Scot 4-6-0 No. 46169 *The Boy Scout* has just dropped onto the table; the balancing operation is obvious by the position of the fireman to the front of the locomotive with the driver looking out of the fireman's side of the cab. On this occasion, perfect balance was achieved at the first attempt.

Opposite: A rare visitor to Patricroft sheds during the early sixties was Stanier Princess Royal Pacific No. 46206 *Princess Marie Louise.* During the rebuilding of Manchester London Road (now Piccadilly) she found her way onto the depot after working a West of England train into Manchester Victoria, then onto Ordsal Lane carriage sidings with the empty stock. A Patricroft crew relieved the wrong train on platform 11 of Victoria, thus explaining the presence of a 'Lizzie' on shed, in spite of the fact that they were banned from running between Salford station and Liverpool Road.

This final night shot features 'Britannia' Pacific No. 70010 *Owen Glendower* photographed on the ash pit at Patricroft after completing a running in turn from Crewe. The tail lamp between the buffers indicates that she has run tender first from Manchester, possibly after working South on the Scottish fish train. An ash wagon and part of the ash plant are visible to the right of shot.

Daylight comes and reveals the fact that No. 70010 has had a full paint up job with no lining out or nameplates in comparison with No. 70050's patch up job (see page 32). No. 70010 is facing west and being positioned for photographs from the coal shute. A Black Five, Patricroft station and the old yard sidings and platforms are visible to the left of shot.

The ultimate photographic position: No. 70010 is posing for J.R.C. who is in a precarious vantage point at the top of the coal shute at Patricroft. The position of the coal empties and Class 8F's tender is unfortunate in the composition, but I hope that this unorthodox view will partly compensate for these deficiencies by also revealing the 'semi-submerged' nature of the sleepers and the typical 'ash' ballast to be found at a motive power depot – modellers again take note.

Another Ex-Crosti Class 9F No. 92025 hard at it on Shap with a Northbound freight train assisted by the Tebay banker which is approaching Scout Green signal box. This book started with a trip on a grimy 9F and I think it is appropriate to finish with one.